Thank You
for Giving Me David...

Linda Edgar DDS MEd

Published by
Hybrid Global Publishing
301 E 57th Street
4th Floor
New York, NY 10022

Manufactured in the United States of America, or in the United
Kingdom when distributed elsewhere.

Edgar, Linda
    Thank You for Giving me David
    LCCN: 2020925588
    ISBN: 978-1-951943-54-7
    eBook: 978-1-951943-55-4

Cover design by: Natasha Clawson
Copyediting by: Lara Kennedy
Interior design by: Suba Murugan

drlinda@edgardds.com

Prologue

This is a story about miracles, loss, sacrifice, hope, and love. I have waited to write this story for over forty years… In life we have our tragedies and our triumphs. Sometimes when we feel we have experienced what might be the worst possible loss in our life—something that rips your heart out and leaves you in a fog, feeling like life is not worth living—suddenly something very positive develops out of that experience. Something allows you to crawl out of the hole you are drowning in and experience the best feeling you could have ever imagined.

I am in my seventh decade of life and have been through several ups and downs. My story is about the loss of two of my children before they were born, two near-death experiences for me in eleven months, and the miracle that occurred in my life five months later. That miracle was the unexpected gift of my newborn son, David.

"I really respect the person who heals a heart they did not break and raises a child they did not make" is one of my favorite sayings.

Please enjoy my story, *Thank You for Giving Me David*.

Chapter 1

During that winter in 1977 when a nineteen-year-old woman walked into Irwin Army Community Hospital in Manhattan, Kansas, and announced that she wanted to give up her baby, my life changed forever. It came after a year of tragedy for my husband Bryan and me, followed by what I felt must have been "God's plan" for me. It is my hope that David's natural mother, who gave our son, born on April 29, 1977, to us will somehow find this small book, *Thank You for Giving Me David*, and find out what her decision to give up her child did for my husband, Bryan, and me.

The saying "Life happens while we are busy making other plans" was certainly true for me. It is my hope that David's natural mother, who we were told was about five feet, nine inches tall and already had two other sons older than David, will discover this story and find out that her decision to give David up for adoption was a good one. He was three days old. She will no longer wonder if David is OK, if he is happy. She will know she made the right choice.

David is a 737 pilot, married for over ten years, with two beautiful daughters. He has worked hard and couldn't be a better father, husband, and son. He is always there for me and always seems to know when I need a visit and some "son time." It is also my hope that my story will highlight "the other side" of adoption.

Often young girls get pregnant and decide to abort their child so that the pregnancy or an unwanted baby does not "ruin" their life plans. Other stories are about a child who was given up at birth only to rediscover their biological parent when they become an adult. Sometimes these are happy reunions, and sometimes the biological parent does not want to be found. They do not want to be reminded of that painful decision they made many years ago.

There are very few stories about the parents who do the adopting and what they have been through before they decide to "raise a child they did not make." There are very few stories about what happened to them that made it impossible to have children naturally.

It is my hope that my story might motivate a young girl who finds herself pregnant by "mistake" to keep her baby, like David's biological mom did. I hope she will consider the many, many women who cannot have their own biological children. It is my hope this young woman would chose to give her child to another woman who cannot have her own babies.

I am not saying a woman should not have a "right to choose" an abortion. I am only trying to give a young pregnant woman who can't see a way to raise a baby another option. I am hoping she will choose to give this miracle of life to another family.

This is a gift like no other.

I have not personally had to choose between aborting or keeping a child in my life, but I can only imagine the hollow and stabbing feeling a person must have when she feels she has to go through this procedure and actually eliminate a human being who could have had a very full life and loving family. It is my final hope this story will motivate a person who finds herself pregnant to choose to have the baby and provide the gift of a lifetime to someone like me. I cannot imagine how different my life would be now if my son had not been "given up" at birth.
As I grow older and have experienced the trials and triumphs of my life, my one desire is to matter to someone and make a difference in the lives of others. "To help heal a heart I did not break and raise a child I did not make." I hope this book will help others.

THE EARLY YEARS

My name is Linda Johansen Edgar. My maiden name was Linda Johansen. I was born in San Diego in August 1951 into a Coast Guard family. I remember Mom telling me her dad had given her a blank check when she got married, to use in case she changed her mind and wanted to come home. For the next seventeen years, we lived all over the United States and half of the world. We moved every two to three years and lived in many places, including Florida; Washington, DC; Virginia; Maryland; the Philippines; Puerto Rico; and finally, Port Angeles, Washington. We moved from Puerto Rico to Port Angeles in Washington State in 1966, my ninth grade year. There were three kids in our family; my two brothers were Bruce, who was eighteen months older than me, and Andrew, who was four years younger. We were all accomplished swimmers, often competing in races on swim teams and open water swims in Puerto Rico.

Port Angeles is a small town about two hours north of Seattle, Washington, by car. When my dad and our family were transferred there from Puerto Rico, my mom said, "We were living in the best place on earth—we are living in heaven."

MEETING BRYAN

In 1967, I was in tenth grade in Port Angeles, minding my own business at swim team practice. To accommodate more swimmers, the lanes were roped off, and the swimmers on the team swam down the left side of the lane and back on the right side of the same lane. I was following the "rules" of lane swimming when this new boy totally ignored the rules and swam smack into me. I found out later this boy's name was Bryan Edgar. Much later, I also found out that he knew the rules of competitive lane swimming, and his goal that day had been to meet me by swimming down the lane the wrong way and crashing into me. The year was 1967, and we quickly became friends, and then more than friends.

He told me I was the girl he planned to be with the rest of his life. I was not sure that was my "plan," however. My dad called Bryan my "friend." Bryan was definitely not my dad's choice for a permanent boyfriend, much less a possible future husband. By then, Dad was a captain and the chief executive officer of the Coast Guard base in Port Angeles. Dad would not even use Bryan's name until we were married several years later. He was very strict and didn't want me getting serious with a boy at such a young age, but Bryan and I were very, very close, and we knew we wanted to get married someday. A year and a half later, in the spring of 1968, right before my senior year in high school, my father received notice that he was going to be transferred again. This time he would be the district commanding officer at the Coast Guard base in San Diego, where he was promoted to admiral.

We had moved every two to three years to a new base. This was normal "military life" but really hard on us kids, especially as we got older and our friends became a bigger part of our lives. We would move to a new city and new schools and make new friends, and as soon as we were "fitting in," we would be transferred, usually quite a distance away. I was devastated when I learned we would be moving from Washington State to California. Bryan would be starting college at Washington State University in Pullman, Washington, and I would have to spend my senior year in high school at a brand new school. We would be separated, and I knew that would make it really hard to keep up a long-distance relationship and that there would be many new college-age girls at Washington State University to tempt him. He was in pre-dentistry and knew he wanted to go to dental school. Dentistry was his passion. Bryan had known since he was in seventh grade that he wanted to be a dentist. I was very mad at my parents for putting me through this move and forcing me to be away from a boy that I loved. I was VERY, VERY lonely.

Bryan and I called and wrote letters to each other every day while he was in Pullman, Washington, and I was in San Diego. I would sneak out to a pay phone and call Bryan when I could so that my dad was not aware. Dad was hoping we would "move on" and forget about each other. Both of us wanted to get married after I graduated from high school in 1969. My school had a Grad Night at Disneyland for all the graduating seniors, and Bryan came down to San Diego for that event. We even went to Tijuana and took a picture under the "Marriages and Divorces" sign.

Linda Graduation

Bryan asked me to marry him at the Grad Night event at Disneyland in Ana-heim, California. Dad said he wouldn't help me with college at all if I was married, and Bryan was paying for college with student loans, so we decided to wait to get married until I finished college. We spent the next four years studying together. Bryan continued to work toward his goal of going to dental school, and I enrolled in courses for pre-med. Bryan and I decided I would apply to teach in the public schools to help pay for him to finish dental school. We decided I would go to medical school after he graduated from dental school in 1976.

BRYAN IN DENTAL SCHOOL AND THE DES SCARE
Bryan was accepted into the University of Washington Dental School in 1972. I had one more year of undergraduate schooling at the University of Washington to finish my zoology and teaching degrees. My parents had been transferred to a new duty station in Portsmouth, Virginia. Dad would be working as the Coast Guard district commander, guarding the coast from

Virginia to Florida. In early 1972, when I was a junior in college at the University of Washington, my mother, Hazel, saw a TV show about a drug called Diethylstilbestrol (DES). She was very interested, because she'd had my brother, Bruce, six weeks early, and her doctor had had her take this drug while she was pregnant with me to help prevent me from being born prematurely.

DES is an estrogen supplement that was supposed to keep women from having miscarriages and premature births. Many doctors prescribed this drug to mothers who were pregnant from 1945 through the 1960s. The TV program my mother had watched was claiming women whose mothers had taken this drug were getting ovarian cancer at a young age, often younger than twenty years old. The same women who were getting ovarian cancer were also having other problems with their reproductive tracts. There were also reports of offspring whose mothers had taken this drug having a hard time getting pregnant.[1]

In some cases, the offspring had endometriosis, which manifested as adhesions around the Fallopian tubes. These adhesions might cause a fertilized egg to get stuck in the tube. Most of the time, the eggs just die, but sometimes the baby grows in the tube to a size that causes the tube to rupture.

I decided to do research on this drug and found that "tubal pregnancies" were reported in about two out of one hundred women who became pregnant and are the reason for 10–15 percent of all deaths in pregnant women. The age group of women most affected was close to my age of twenty to twenty-five years old, which correlated with the ages that the TV program said this ovarian cancer often showed up. If the mother had taken DES while she was pregnant, cancer and pregnancy problems usually occurred in the daughter when she was nineteen to twenty-nine years old. My mother called me right after she watched this show, terrified that I might have ovarian cancer or other problems. I had never had a lot of trouble with my monthly periods. My periods were every twenty-eight

---

[1] Josie L. Tenove, MD SM, "Ectopic Pregnancy," *American Family Physician 61*, no. 4 (2000): 1080–1088.

days, very regular, and I had never used birth control. I had started menstruation a few years earlier than normal at the age of ten. My mother's phone call really scared me, so I got checked by a gynecologist at the University of Washington right away.

Nothing cancerous showed up in the pap smear, except that cells from my pap smear were not stage one but classified as stage two. This meant the cells could be precancerous. It was suggested by my doctor that I get a biopsy of my cervix just to be sure. In a cervical biopsy, the doctor takes a punch out of the cervix without any anesthesia to check for cancer. Basically, they cut tissue out of your cervix to test it for cancer or precancer cells. Class two cells showed up again when they checked this biopsy. The doctor suggested that I get this test done every year to check my cellular growth. This kind of biopsy was very painful for me, and I was not looking forward to these checkups, although I did follow through and get them done regularly. It never occurred to me that a drug my mother took when she was pregnant with me might cause me problems twenty years later on in life, when I was trying to have children.

BRYAN'S PROPOSAL

In 1972, Bryan was in his first year of dental school. I was in my fourth year of undergraduate college at the University of Washington. As with all young couples, we had our arguments throughout our six-year courtship. He was living in the dorm and busy studying for dental school. I was living in the dorms and working hard to keep my grades up so I could get into medical school, become an OBGYN, and deliver babies. It was hard to find time to be together. It seemed as if Bryan had forgotten we had talked about getting married when I graduated from high school but decided to put it off until I finished undergraduate college. During my senior year at the University of Washington, we rarely talked about it anymore.

We visited Port Angeles one weekend in late summer of 1972 to see Bryan's mom. Bryan asked me to drive with him up to the top of Hurricane Ridge, which is a beautiful viewing point at the top of a mountain in the Olympic National

Park, seventeen miles south of Port Angeles. I was just about ready to break up with him that day. We had been together for six years and had planned to get married, but lately everything had been about Bryan's needs, and we never seemed to talk about our future plans anymore. I realized that dental school was stressful and all-consuming, so I had been patient, but if we were going to get married when I graduated the following June, I needed some time to plan the wedding. This could have been our romantic time alone, but Bryan had decided to ask a friend to go up to the top of the mountain with us. The scenery from the top of Hurricane Ridge was as close as you get to heaven. In the middle of our hike, just before sunset, with the birds flying around and singing and the wildflowers in bloom, Bryan got down on one knee. My stomach cramped; I could tell he was shaking—and he asked me to marry him. Then I started shaking—REALLY shaking. This was a shock!

It was the last thing I had expected—he had been thinking about marriage after all, he just wanted it to be a surprise. The reason he asked his friend to come up with us was so he wouldn't have to do the driving back down the mountain, thinking he would be too emotional. And we were both VERY emotional. We had waited a long six years for this moment. To this day, I am not sure if Bryan knew I had planned to break up with him that day. We set the date to get married about nine months later, June 23, 1973, just a few weeks after I was to graduate from the University of Washington. We decided to have the wedding in Port Angeles, Washington, since Bryan's parents and most of our friends lived there. My parents still lived in Portsmouth, Virginia, and they planned to retire there. We were able to book the Coast Guard Officers Club on the "spit" at Ediz Hook in Port Angeles for the reception. I can't remember if Bryan had asked my dad's permission to marry me. Dad at that point was still calling Bryan "your friend" whenever we talked about him.

THE WEDDING, JUNE 23, 1973

Mom organized the wedding long-distance. She made all six bridesmaid's dresses while living in Portsmouth and organized the whole wedding at the Methodist Church in Port Angeles, Washington, from across the country.

Bryan and Linda Wedding

SUMMER 1973

That summer, I lifeguarded and managed the Sequim pool, which is about a half hour east of Port Angeles, and Bryan worked in the plywood mill to help save money for dental school. I did not have any ovarian cancer scares during that year but did get a yearly pap smear to be sure. My cells would always be in the class two range. I began to worry about what this "class two" description really meant, but none of my gynecologists explained anything to me.

I remember budgeting to buy a gallon of ice cream once a month for $1.75, and we existed on popcorn, potatoes, and tuna fish. Bryan was in his second year of dental school, trying to pay for tuition, books, and supplies. We qualified for married student housing located only a few blocks from the dental school. The "apartment" was tiny—only about three hundred square feet. But you could not beat the $75-a-month rent. The bathroom was large enough to stand up in, with a very small shower we shared with the cockroaches.

We decided that I would teach and wait to go to medical school until after Bryan graduated from dental school and had finished his two-year residency in Kansas. By the end of the summer, Bryan got word that he had received an army scholarship that paid for tuition and a small stipend. This was a huge relief. With this news, we felt like we were "rich"!

OUR FIRST HOME PURCHASE

We saved our money for a year and were able to buy a house one mile from the University of Washington Dental School. We met some wonderful neighbors, Bob and Linda Williams, and also had many close friends through our dental school Bible study fellowship groups. Life was busy and hard, but we were happy and working toward our dreams.

BRYAN'S SENIOR YEAR, 1975–1976

In the fall of 1975, Bryan's senior year in dental school, I had been having cramps for several months, sometimes VERY severe. This was extremely unusual for me, since I usually have a very high pain threshold. I was an athlete—a runner and a swimmer—and was used to hard workouts and pain from sore muscles. I was incredibly tired, and my stomach was bloating. I was teaching science and would double over in pain in the middle of a lab and have to leave my classroom and lie down.

I had never had pain with my periods, so I went to my gynecologist to get checked. I was VERY scared. What was happening to me? I thought back to my mother's phone call about the DES two years ago. I was working on my master of science education degree and had asked to do research on DES. I made the mistake of mentioning to the OBGYN during my appointment that I wanted to go to medical school and study to be an OBGYN myself. I told the doctor about my history of being a "DES baby," or someone whose mother had taken this drug when she was pregnant with me. I was twenty-four years old, and I was afraid it might be ovarian cancer or this pain might be related to my DES history. I told him about my research. The doctor looked at me and rolled his eyes, indicating to me that he didn't think I knew what I was talking about.

The doctor palpated my abdomen, which was very swollen and painful, and came up with nothing. He asked me very little about my health history and did not develop a differential diagnosis. All he had to tell me was, "Girls should not go to medical school. You aren't strong enough. This is probably just a bad period." He spent about ten minutes with me. No X-rays or ultrasounds were taken. He found nothing and said it was all in my head. He said I needed to be tougher. "If you can't handle a little discomfort, you will NEVER make it through medical school," he exclaimed.

His examination of me was not thorough, and I was very angry when I left his office. I was not only angry, but I was VERY HURT. He did NOT know me at all. He talked AT me and did not listen to me. He dismissed my history of DES, calling it nonsense, even though studies I had read were well-documented in the research literature and in medical journals. He was only interested in rushing me out of his office. So I put up with the pain for several more months. From September through December, severe pains—GUT-WRENCHING pains—would stab me in the abdomen with such force that I suddenly doubled over and had to leave my classroom. In hindsight, I should have gotten a second opinion when things didn't improve and seemed to be getting worse.

BRYAN'S DAD DIES OF A HEART ATTACK

In December of Bryan's senior year of dental school in 1975, we got an urgent call from Bryan's mom. Bryan's father had died suddenly of a heart attack in his sleep just before Christmas. We had been married about a year and a half. We dropped everything and left Seattle immediately to drive up to Port Angeles. We comforted Bryan's mom and his three younger brothers. His dad had died so suddenly and unexpectedly. Bryan was the oldest, and he and his cousins from Canada helped with the funeral arrangements. I continued to have severe pain throughout the funeral and could hardly stand up without doubling over in pain. I was tired all the time. I thought the severe pain and fatigue might be from stress. This was not at all like me. While we were at the funeral for Bryan's dad, my breasts were very tender, and all I wanted to do was get back to the house and sleep.

We had a lot of "life decisions" to be made in a short time. We were waiting for orders from the army to see where we would be transferred in the next six months for Bryan's dental residency. I was teaching all day and finishing up my master of science education at night. My junior high classes were very full, and I had a few students who had been advanced to junior high because the teachers couldn't handle their behavior at the elementary level. I left my teaching day exhausted, with a clenched jaw and tight shoulders, almost every day. So, naturally, I thought maybe the stomach pains were just stress. It had been a tough first year of marriage, and Bryan had the added stress of losing his dad suddenly and finishing his requirements to graduate from dental school. It never occurred to me I might be pregnant.

NEW YEAR'S EVE 1976: THE FIRST DISASTER

We tried to put that year behind us, so we decided to celebrate the new year in 1976 by having a New Year's Eve party at our house, even though I had not been feeling well. We invited our medical and dental school friends from our Bible study to come. That evening, I barely finished making the food and felt weak and nauseated. I went into the bathroom and tried to throw up. The pain on New Year's Eve was so intense I could not sit or stand without feeling like I was going to faint. I had been having terrible, severe intermittent pain with cramping for the last several months. I ended up back in the bathroom—almost fainting—while everyone else was celebrating the new year. I definitely felt better when I was lying down flat. Our friends at the party thought I had just come down with a virus.

I called the gynecologist on call, and once again he said it was probably just a bad period. I tried to explain to him that I did not typically have trouble with my periods and I felt like something must be wrong! You could tell he was impatient to end the call. Frustrated once again, I just hung up. Every time I tried to sit up, I started to faint and felt nauseated. I began to have excruciating pain in my stomach, even worse than I had had before. It was like someone was stabbing me with a knife. I was sweating profusely. My stomach was distended and getting more so...

I was surrounded by medical and dental school friends who had come to the party, and no one could figure out what was wrong with me.

We finally decided to call 911. It was New Year's Eve, so 911 was very busy with accidents and drug overdoses. The ambulance finally came and rushed me to Bellevue Overlake Medical Center, about half an hour away.

In the ambulance, the EMTs could not get an IV inserted. My blood pressure usually ran a little high, 140 over 90, so the blood pressure reading was not exceptionally low (100/60), but it was low for my normal baseline measure. My vision was blurry. It was New Year's Eve and there were several overdose cases in the ER when we arrived at Overlake Medical Center. Since I did not appear to be critical, I was pushed off to the side. Bryan was not allowed to come into the emergency room with me.

The emergency room doctor FINALLY came over to see me. By then I was semiconscious. Finally, the doctor actually listened to my symptoms and thought the symptoms might be more than me just having a bad period. He realized the fainting and pain might mean there was some internal bleeding. Much of what was being said was fuzzy, and I felt like I was going unconscious.

I remember the doctor doing a punch biopsy through my abdomen, where the doctor basically punches a hole in your stomach to see if there is internal bleeding. Now THAT woke me up, as blood spurted out of the hole like a geyser. Although I was not really conscious, I heard the doctor scream, "Tell Dr. Kettering to get his butt in here, FAST!" Dr. Kettering was the OBGYN who had found nothing wrong with me three months earlier. He was on call that night. He was the one who said I couldn't make it in medical school because I was not "tough enough." He was the one who dismissed my symptoms and did not do tests to find a condition that is one of the top reasons women die who are pregnant and have ruptured tubal pregnancies.

I later learned ectopic or tubal pregnancies are the most common cause of death among women during their first trimester. About 5 percent of women have a tubal pregnancy. Often the baby dies, but in my case, it had been growing within the Fallopian tube, which accounted for the cramping that had been increasing during the previous two months. Bryan and my neighbors Linda and Bob did not know what was going on as they wheeled me into the operating room. All Bryan could do was look through the emergency room window. He was watching as they rolled me into emergency surgery to try to stop the bleeding.

At the time, neither of us knew how close I was to dying.

The cramping had also occurred because I had a cyst growing on one of my ovaries. The cyst had ruptured. I was pregnant, but the baby had been caught in the tube, and it had grown larger than the tube could stretch, causing the Fallopian tube to rupture. This is called an ectopic pregnancy.

The tube with the growing fetus usually ruptures between six weeks and three months. The ovary and whole tube had to be removed. The doctor said I was lucky, that I had lost half my blood by the time they figured it out and I had nearly died.

Lucky??? I thought. We were told it would be harder to get pregnant with only one tube and one ovary. My minister came by to visit, and he said, "God only gives you trials you can handle. This will make you stronger." One thing it certainly did was help me understand the pain and feeling of loss and depression any woman who has a miscarriage goes through, and later on I was able to help other friends through similar tough experiences. I also wondered, *What is wrong with me? Did I do something to cause this?* It had never occurred to me that I would have trouble with pregnancies... I had lots of questions... but no real answers.

We were advised by the doctor who did my surgery not to wait and that we should try to get pregnant again right away. To this day, I have never understood why this doctor, who had incorrectly diagnosed me in the first place, didn't suggest that I get some kind of tests done to see if there may be problems with the other Fallopian tube before I tried to get pregnant again?

14

Clearly his only advice was to try again, and soon.

I was twenty-four years old. I REALLY wanted to have children, and Bryan was finishing his senior year in dental school. I took six weeks off from teaching because I'd had to have a C-section to remove the damaged tube, baby, and ovary and stop the hemorrhaging blood. The scar across my belly reminded me daily about not only the physical pain but the emotional pain of losing a child and the thought of never being able to have children of my own. It is really tough, mentally, to go through a C-section and not have a baby to show for it.

Many of my friends were pregnant or having their second child. Several pregnant friends came to see me while I was recovering, which was very difficult for me. They did not realize it was hard for me to see them pregnant. When I did see them, sometimes I felt like less of a woman because I could not give my husband a child. It was VERY hard to go into the OBGYN office and see the pregnant young women and remember the pain I had just gone through. Every time I went for a checkup at the OBGYN's office, I relived that awful night. I usually ended up crying. My scar, which traversed my whole lower stomach, reminded me daily of the loss of what could have been our first child.

My mom flew to Seattle from Virginia to help take care of me. She had a heart attack later that year, and I often thought it may have been the stress of what happened to me and losing the baby that caused the attack.

We never really discussed it, but instinctively I knew she blamed herself, because she took the DES while she was pregnant with me. She thought this loss was somehow her fault.

A NEW LIFE IN KANSAS DENTAL ARMY RESIDENCY
In the spring of 1976, Bryan and I found out we would be going to Kansas, to the Irwin Army Community Hospital, for Bryan's dental residency. We would leave at the end of the summer and drive down to Kansas in our lime-green Volkswagen van. I retired from my teaching job in Washington and had applied to do research

Lime-green Volkswagen van

First house in Kansas

at Kansas State University. We bought a small house in Manhattan, Kansas, in a neighborhood where all the houses were the same. I remembered the doctor had told us after my first ruptured tubal pregnancy that if we wanted to have children, we should try right away. Bryan threw himself into his residency responsibilities, and I was busy at Kansas State University trying to find a nitrogen-fixing bacteria to help with the petroleum problem.

We also worked on getting pregnant… a lot. We timed my cycles and made getting pregnant a priority. My hours at the lab streaking agar plates and using the gas chromatography machine were much less stressful than teaching five different classes of thirty-five junior high students each. In October, nine months after losing our first baby and having my first tubal, I was in the research lab and began having the same symptoms I had had before when the baby got caught in the tube. I was using the gas chromatography machine in the lab, and once again I suddenly had knife-stabbing pains in my stomach, causing me to double over in pain. The pain would dissipate and then come back with a vengeance.

Once again I went to the doctor, and after talking to me for a few minutes, he found nothing wrong. Once again this gynecologist did not consider my history of DES or the recent tubal pregnancy. ("They are so rare," he said.) He did not do much of an exam or any kind of ultrasound. My breasts felt sore. We did a pregnancy test, which came out negative. After doing my own research, I later found out that although I did not get ovarian cancer at a young age, DES had also been found to have possible correlation with a condition some women have called endometriosis, which can cause binding of the Fallopian tubes. Often women who have tubal pregnancies have this binding that prevents the egg from getting up the Fallopian tube into the uterus. When my symptoms continued, I told the gynecologist about these studies, but he shook his head in disbelief. Physicians really hate it when you try to diagnose yourself.

THE SECOND DISASTER (NIGHT BEFORE THANKSGIVING)
About a month later, I collapsed on the bathroom floor right outside the lab where I was doing research at Kansas State. The stabbing pain was worse than I

had ever felt before, and I was very light-headed. My husband was in his residency class somewhere, and we could not find him. I was in excruciating pain—it was getting worse—and I was feeling very faint. The ceiling was spinning, and I was beginning to pass out. It was eleven months after we discovered my first tubal pregnancy in Seattle, which had happened on New Year's Eve 1975. I was now twenty-five years old, and it was the night before Thanksgiving in 1976. I called my neighbor, who helped me into her station wagon so I could lie down flat in the back and not pass out. Once again, I was bleeding internally and had not been diagnosed. She rushed me to the emergency room.

The same thing was happening all over again. The pain was unbearable. I was rushed into surgery. While I was being rolled in for emergency surgery on the gurney, I remember a doctor saying, "You might as well have it all out; you can't have kids anyway." Even though I was barely conscious, I still remember those very painful words, spoken by someone who had no empathy for my condition and, in my opinion, should NOT be a doctor. I fainted, and that is all I remembered until the next day. That doctor's cruel statement to a twenty-five-year-old girl fighting for her life is stuck in my memory like it was spoken to me yesterday. The next day, I woke up and felt tremendous pain again in my abdomen. They had done a second Cesarean surgery in eleven months. They cut me open again through the same scar and removed the baby and damaged tube but were able to save part of my remaining ovary.

The same thing had happened... again. The baby had gotten caught in the tube and did not make it to the uterus. This may have been why the pregnancy tests were negative. My second child had died. Even now as I write this story, I cry—the loss I felt was unbearable. Another minister came in again and said, "God only gives you what you can handle." I couldn't imagine what that meant. I had lost my second tube but still had an ovary, so I did not have to go on estrogen replacement therapy. My emotions were on "high alert."

The doctor had said, "Try again right away to get pregnant." We did, and it failed. I was twenty-five years old and realized I would never be able to have my own children naturally. About 6.1 million women, or about 10 percent of women in the United States, have trouble getting pregnant for various reasons. It was 1976. At that time, all the procedures like implanting a fetus and using a surrogate were not well established. We could not have afforded any of those procedures anyway. All I knew was that I would never physically be able to have a baby.

I cried almost every day. I love children and had wanted to have several. I asked God, "Why me? What did I do wrong? I have always been a good person. I would have made a great mother... Why do other people who don't even want to have kids get pregnant so easily? Why do people who mistreat their kids get pregnant so easily?" Seeing my friends who were pregnant nearly destroyed me, and I fell into a deep depression. Our neighborhood was full of young military wives, most of whom were pregnant. It was torture for me. I felt terribly inadequate as a woman. I was not able to do what was so natural for others. I was smart and athletic, having been a competitive swimmer all my life. I took care of myself...

Why me? I would ask over and over. At first I began to lose my faith in God—but I had many good friends, like Linda Williams, Rembie Krattli, and Linda Donaldson, who stood by and supported me during this tough time of loss. We went through a lot together, and they are still close friends today. I had to go back into the gynecologist's office to get checked regularly. Sitting in the reception area with all the pregnant women in the waiting room was unbearable. I broke down in tears before and after almost every appointment. Small children with their parents were everywhere. All of my neighbors had children. I could not understand why God was making it so hard for me to do what comes so naturally to so many people.

A VERY SUPPORTIVE HUSBAND
I knew Bryan had wanted kids of our own, and I did not know whether he would want to divorce me and find someone he could have his own biological children with. He was very positive. He stuck with me. Bryan was busy with his dental residency at Irwin Army Community Hospital, and I finally decided, after the

first of that year in 1977, that God had given me this path for a reason, and even though I did not understand what God was doing with me, perhaps he had another plan.

I went back to the lab and threw myself into research. It was January 1977, and we were in the middle of the gas crisis. Cars were lined up at the pumps to try to get their share of gas. We were working on isolating a nitrogen-fixing bacteria to help with the petroleum and gas crisis. I read books like *The Baby Trap* to make myself feel better—these books emphasized the positives of not having children. I refocused and realized it was my turn now to go back to school. I decided with this horrible tubal pregnancy experience that being an OBGYN would probably be too tough for me emotionally, so I decided to apply to dental schools. I took the Dental Admission Test and began to get my credentials and recommendations in order.

"It is much better not to have kids," I told myself. "Think of the benefits." After about three months, I was starting to feel positive about life again. Psychologically, I was trying to protect myself. Bryan was finishing up his dental residency in Kansas, and we would be heading back to Seattle the following year, so it was a perfect time to apply to the University of Washington Dental School.

In the winter of 1977, a few months after I had lost the second baby, Bryan was told about the hospital's "in-house adoption list" by one of the doctors who knew I had lost my second baby in eleven months. Bryan was doing his anesthesia rotation, and he'd decided to put our name on an in-house adoption list but had forgotten to tell me about it. I think subconsciously he had not told me because he didn't want to get my hopes up. I had given up ever becoming a "natural" mom, and we had never even considered adoption. It was too expensive. Four months later, in early April 1977, I was in the lab doing research on nitrogen-fixing bacteria when Bryan called me. He never called during the day. My hope was that nothing was wrong. It had been quite a year—a most devastating year. When I answered the phone, Bryan was very excited and said, "How would you like to have a baby?" The comment stabbed me through my heart, because it had been hard to get past the fact that I could not naturally have children, when it came so easily to so many other people.

I answered Bryan sharply, "I am not ready to kid about this."

He said, "No, no, listen—there is a girl that came into the hospital today and wants to give up her baby! I just got the call. They want to know if we are interested."

My heart immediately fell into my stomach.

I had talked myself into the advantages of not having children over the last three months, and my mind was VERY confused. I told Bryan I would need to think about it. For the last three months, to protect myself psychologically, I had looked for all the reasons it was best NOT to have children, and now I was faced with this development!

"The baby is due in seven days, so they asked us to decide right away," Bryan said. "Let's talk about it when I get home."

I went home from the lab early in a daze and immediately told my neighbor, who was pregnant with her second child, about the possibility of an adoption—in seven days!

She was so excited. She was the one who had driven me to the hospital when I lost the second baby, and she was with me when I sank into a deep depression, knowing I could not have my own natural child.

I thought this must be some kind of miracle. Maybe this was God's plan for us.

Bryan got home that night from his classes so excited. We talked late into the night and decided to say yes to the baby. The next morning, we received another piece of news. The baby was not due in seven days. The baby was due to be born on the seventh of April, which was in twenty-four hours! I was so excited I let go of all the "baby trap" ideas I had hung onto after losing our two babies. I purchased Doctor Spock's *Baby and Child Care* the next day and made a baby quilt that night. I was so excited I couldn't sleep.

We waited in anticipation of what we believed was a *miracle* for us.

We had lost two babies, which made us feel even more thankful for the possibility of giving this new little baby our love and our life.

It never occurred to me to ask any questions about the baby's mother or father. Had she taken care of herself while she was pregnant? Our neighbors, who had small children, helped me out with a VERY fast course on what you needed to be a mom. We went to garage sales and got set up that weekend with a used crib, formula, cloth diapers, bottle warmer, onesies, toys, and a swing. We were waiting each day for the call. *What if she changed her mind?* A week went by… no baby yet. I was so nervous and excited that I was visibly shaking.

I found out she was nineteen years old and had already had two boys at age sixteen and eighteen that were currently living with their grandparent. The birth mother's marriage was not doing well.

THE WAIT

Two weeks went by and no baby. Every day we had to wait, we got more excited, anticipating this new little baby… We hoped so much that she wasn't going to change her mind.

Finally, on April 29, 1977, we got the call. He was three weeks late! We were told that a healthy, brand-new eight-pound, two-ounce baby boy—nineteen inches long—had been born. We had to wait THREE LONG DAYS before we could pick him up at the hospital. My heart rate was constantly elevated with excitement and the anticipation of finally holding this new "little one" in our arms.

There was still a chance that his natural mother or her parents would decide to keep the baby. We hired a lawyer and asked for a closed adoption, so names

Bryan with our new SON the first day home from the hospital

were not exchanged. We did ask the mother to give us a letter describing any health issues in the family. We found out the mother was blonde with blue eyes; five feet, nine inches tall; and weighed 150 pounds. No information was given to us about the dad. This is all we knew of the reason the natural mother had decided to give up our son. I am SO glad she did not get an abortion. She already had had two sons. Now she was nineteen, having her third baby and needing to make a very tough decision. I was twenty-five and Bryan had just turned twenty-seven.

THE GIFT

We were young and poor, with a lot of debt from school, but we had a lot of love and a great potential future to give our new son.

I prayed deep in my heart that the grandparents would not want to raise David. I don't know if I could have taken another huge disappointment. The mother did not change her mind, and I was holding my breath—floating on air—and could not stop smiling. This must certainly be the miracle God had in mind for us. An unbelievable year after losing two babies and losing Bryan's dad—could this miracle really be happening? Three days after the birth, our lawyer picked up our new son from the hospital and handed him to us—an unbelievable miracle. I was shaking with happiness and fear at the same time, not knowing quite what to do with a brand-new baby. The picture on the front cover of this book is David the day we brought him home from the hospital.

I had never thought about the "Pro-Life" political movement until we went through this experience, but I am so glad that this biological mother did not abort my son. We paid our lawyer two hundred dollars for her time. Because the birth mother was a military wife, all the costs of the hospitalization and delivery were covered. Our lawyer drew up the papers and said there would be a waiting period for the adoption to be final. The state of Kansas has one of the shortest waiting periods of any state for adopting a child (thank goodness!).

And so, Bryan and I went home to start our new adventure. A name—we had not picked out a name… We thought of the name David because of the story of David and Goliath and how David overcame insurmountable odds… Robert, his middle name, was after our very good friend Robert Williams, who remains close to us today. There was no better feeling than putting our brand-new son on our chest, lying down, and watching him sleep.

THE FIRST SIX WEEKS
Bryan was gone most of the time with his residency classes and projects. My professor in the lab said I could bring David to work with me as long as I could get my work done. For the first two weeks, you think you have a perfect baby, and then the truth "kicks in." I decided to work 6:00 a.m. to 10:00 a.m., go home during the middle of the day, and come back and work 6:00 p.m. to 10:00 p.m. My plan was that David might sleep during these shifts in the lab. Unfortunately, my schedule for David was not his schedule for me. He ended up with a bad case of colic and screamed, it seemed, almost twenty-four hours a day. Colic is when an

David 3 months

otherwise healthy baby cries or fusses frequently for no clear reason, often starting at the second week. It is usually the worst between four to six weeks of age. I did not know what to do.

When you adopt a baby in Kansas, it is not final for six weeks, to give time for anyone who might object. This is actually a very short amount of time compared to other states. The social worker in charge of the case shows up, usually unannounced. No matter what I did, David screamed most of the time and seemed to have an insatiable appetite… He was hungry all the time, but every time he ate, he was very uncomfortable and burped up a lot of gas.

With all the crying, I was sure I had "flunked motherhood" and I should give David back to someone who knew what they were doing. I took him to the doctor to see if there was a problem, and they suggested putting him on a straight water

David at three months and Linda with David by Volkswagen van

diet, in case he was allergic to milk. David let me know very quickly that he was not having anything to do with this water diet!

We finally found out he was indeed allergic to milk and put him on a soy-based diet. What a huge difference that made! Once we got the diet figured out, we watched David grow at an exceptionally fast pace. We realized how big David was when his godparents, Robert and Linda Williams, brought my three-month-old goddaughter, Shayna, down to visit us from Seattle. At six weeks, David was bigger than Shayna was at three months old.

Bryan got orders to go back to Seattle and work at Fort Lewis to pay back the three-year scholarship the army had awarded him during dental school. We packed David up at three months old and headed back to Seattle from Manhattan, Kansas, in our lime-green Volkswagen van. Needless to say, my goal of going back to dental school had been put on the back burner.

ANOTHER MAJOR DECISION

In 1977, there were only a few women in a dental class of one hundred, and very few of them had tried to have babies at the same time as they were going through dental school. Now it is very different. Dental school classes are made up of 50 percent women or more, and several women have managed to have babies while they are in school. Some amazing women even have them the week they are taking their state boards. With very supportive husbands and families, this is possible, but in the 1970s, it was frowned upon by some to have children while you were in dental school. Getting into the University of Washington Dental School was tough, and I did not want to go out of state and be split up with my husband, so I only wanted to apply to that school. It was even frowned upon to be a women in dentistry, because many male dentists felt that women weren't strong enough to handle the stress. You can just imagine how THAT comment made me feel.

When we arrived in Federal Way, we stayed with some friends, Mike and Rembie Krattli, while we looked for a place to stay and tried to find a home to buy. My plan was to stay home and take care of David, who was about three months old by then. Money would be tight, but Bryan had his army pay and would be doing dentistry at Fort Lewis. We were asked to house-sit for a friend who was a teacher in the Auburn School District. Our friend, Bill Arrigoni, came home early because his boat broke down. He'd found out there was a math and science teaching job opening at Cascade Junior High School, where he taught, and he asked me if I was interested in applying for the job. I decided to go ahead and go to the interview. What did I have to lose? Another miracle was about to occur.

The principal of Cascade Junior High was the father of some friends we had met in a Bible study group in dental school. I had also received a recommendation from the father of one of my best friends, Jackie Sherris, who had been in our wedding four years earlier. That father was now the superintendent of schools. The stars seemed to line up and indicated to me that I should take this teaching opportunity if it was offered to me. We had also picked out a new house to buy in Federal Way, which was about thirty minutes from the junior high school where the job opening was. It was August 1977. We did not have a phone yet, and cell phones had not been invented, but my friend Rembie drove thirty minutes from her house to Federal Way to let me know I had a second interview with the principal.

When the principal found out the superintendent's daughter was a close friend of mine, it helped to seal the deal. I got the job. It is indeed a small world. Suddenly, I had to prepare to switch from being a "stay-at-home mom" to having to prepare for a new teaching job! Now I had a new challenge. I had a four-month-old AND a new full-time teaching job as a science teacher and track coach that started in three days. I had no one to babysit David. I was about to try to attempt the impossible. Once again, miracles seemed to be on our side. The year before, I had lost two babies. That was one of the worst years of my life. I was twenty-five years old and knew I could not have children of my own—a devastating year. The year to follow was turning out to be one of the best I could have ever imagined.

I am finding out in life that when one door closes and you feel lower and more depressed than you can ever imagine… if you are patient enough, another door often opens. "Tragedies often lead to triumphs." So I started looking for babysitters in our neighborhood. The first door I knocked on in the neighborhood opened to a woman with a bright smile who knew of a wonderful woman who babysat children in her home just down the street. I said a prayer as I walked down the street to her home. The second door I knocked on was that wonderful woman, named Doris, who babysat children, and said she would love to watch David for me during the week while I was teaching junior high science and math. I would also be coaching softball and track. David would be one of several children Doris took care of, but he was the only baby.

She lived two blocks from our house. I asked for references from her, which were glowing. All this came together in less than a week, and it did seem like God had a plan for our lives! Another miracle! A WONDERFUL plan was developing. School was to begin in three days, and I had five different classes to prepare for and teach.

Linda and David, age four months, in front of their new home, September 1977

So I put the idea of going to dental school on the back burner and decided to be a mom and pursue my teaching career. David thrived in his new environment with his "big brothers and sisters" at Doris's house, who loved him dearly. It was very hard leaving a baby every day—I always felt torn and guilty—but Doris was wonderful with David, and I seemed to be a better, possibly more patient mother because I worked during the day. I had a student in one of my ninth grade classes that had never been told he was adopted until he was in my class at the age of fourteen. The year he was told, he went from being an A student to not caring about anything, and he began to flunk my class. It seemed to really hurt him to have this idea that he was adopted sprung on him suddenly. I talked to him about my experience adopting David, which seemed to help him. I shared with him how special he was because his adoptive parents chose him and loved him as their own.

Having that experience made me vow to be up-front with David about how lucky we were to have been able to adopt him and have him in our life. I explained to

David, age eleven months, with Great-Grandmother Ruth

him that sometimes a natural mother can't take care of a new baby for many reasons, and his mother unselfishly decided he would be better off if she let someone else raise him. By age ten, David was approaching my height, and it was pretty obvious that I wasn't his natural mother, although most people did not question the fact that he was our natural son because he had blond hair and blue eyes like mine. Adopting David made me very protective of him.

When David was eleven months old, we decided to take our first trip on an airplane with him. Most people might try a thirty-minute trip first, but we decided to fly six hours to Florida to see my Grandmother Johansen, David's great-grandmother. We decided to take the red-eye so David would sleep. Well, that did not happen, but the people around us were patient with this new baby. We made it, and he had his first experience of Florida in Pompano Beach, eight miles from Fort Lauderdale.

DAVID, YEAR TWO

At one year old, David was in size two clothes. He did not walk until he was fourteen months old, partly because he was so big. He was always off the charts for height. He was not talking at fourteen months, either, except for a few words. I worried like a new mother always does about whether he might be deaf. Was there something more I could be doing?

He slowly began putting words together into sentences. My goddaughter, Shayna, who was six weeks older than David, was talking up a storm by fourteen months, and that was all I had to compare it to. At about two and a half, he was making up for lost time, and he talked nonstop—especially when I was trying to have a phone conversation. At two years old, he was in size four clothes. It is said that if you double a child's height at two years old, you may get close to their projected adult height, which would have placed him at about six feet, six inches.

Life was good. Bryan had three years to pay back the army for his scholarship in dental school, and he was busy looking for an associate dental position in Federal

David at age two

Way. David was always smiling and happy and loved to share his toys. He played with the He-Man figures and Care Bears, especially Rainbow Bear, when he was a toddler. David was so athletic and tall, he crawled out of his crib at age two. He loved to take things apart and watch the airplanes. He was also a BIG flirt, even at age two, and constantly wanted to be with people.

We had installed an aboveground pool in the backyard. One day I had put David down for a nap. I was in the backyard weeding, looked up, and saw him standing there. Because I had been a lifeguard, I knew it was easy for kids to drown in backyard pools—this scared me to death. He came around the corner with a big smile on his face and twinkling eyes. It was really tough to get mad at him! "Mommy, I did it!" he said, so proud of himself! Once again, he had climbed out of his crib. How can you get mad at that face? He was such a cutie! However, we did put a lock on the outside of his bedroom door to keep him "safe."

David hated to go to bed, no matter how tired he was. I used to go in and read him stories—"Just one more," he would say. To calm him down and get him to

David near pool area and Linda with David

David and Shayna Age 3

sleep, I would rub his forehead or his arm lightly to get him to relax, and he would drift off to sleep. He loved Dr. Seuss and a book called *Why Was I Adopted?* He was a really cute toddler, full of smiles and twinkles in his eyes. He didn't want to go to sleep because he didn't want to miss out on anything. David was curious and not afraid of much, except swimming.

At three years old, David decided to take a field trip down the neighborhood onto a busy street—on his own. I literally took my eyes off him for less than a minute, and he was gone to our neighborhood 7-11. When I realized he was gone, I screamed for him and ran down the road. When I caught up to him, I looked him in the eye, and he said he was "exploring." He loved to play hide-and-seek and hide in the clothes racks in the mall. It became a game to him… one that drove me crazy. Although I never got a harness for him, I probably should have! I had put myself through college as a swim instructor, and I tried to teach David to swim at age two, but it wasn't his goal to learn until he was about six years old.

David in the backyard pool age 2

He did love the pool, as long as he had his "floaties." I started competing in running when David was eighteen months old in 1978, and he loved to go to 10k races and cheer for Mom and Dad.

RUNNING, TEACHING, AND RAISING DAVID

Rembie Krattli encouraged me to start running to lose weight a year after David was born, in 1978. I entered a 10k race, which took me about fifty-eight minutes to complete. I was teaching junior high and had a fourteen-year-old student named Trish who had a very bad home life. She was very mature for her age and was basically caring for herself most of the time because her dad was on drugs. She was very responsible and getting all As, and I felt that if she had a home, she might blossom even more. I invited her to live with us, and she watched David when I got up at 5:00 a.m. to run before school. Part of me thinks that I started competing in running because I lost the babies and could not have kids. I might have felt I needed to continue to prove my worth. No matter what I did, it never seemed to be enough.

David , Linda and Bryan after a marathon

David with Grandpa Joe

In 1980, David was three years old and in preschool. He loved to socialize with the other kids but was too active to really sit down and read. He loved the books *The Little Engine That Could* and Dr. Seuss's *The Cat in the Hat*. We decided to go to Disneyland when David was three.

David continued to grow at a very rapid rate, and by age four, he was already in a size eight in clothes. In 1981, when David was four years old, I was asked to transfer to Auburn High School to teach chemistry and coach track. I had been running extensively, averaging about 110 miles a week, from 1980 to 1981.

I would work out with the cross country and track teams, and then, after practice, I ran the eight miles back home from Auburn to Federal Way. David would come with me when we did 10k races or marathons almost every weekend, sometimes on both Saturday and Sunday. He was four years old, and Bryan or Trish would watch him when I went out to do twenty-mile training runs. Bryan was also a runner and cyclist but was a huge supporter and a great father, which allowed me

David on Daytona Beach

David hiking with Dad (Bryan) and Grandpa Joe

David, age three, chowing down after the Seaside, Oregon, marathon

David, age 4 with Buffy –Linda's Parent's Dog

to progress as a runner. I was winning races almost every weekend by then, with first-place prizes of trips to Hawaii and to Europe, which we all enjoyed. I was still teaching full-time. We went to Hawaii as a family several times using these "Trip Awards." We also flew as a family to Daytona Beach every year and back to Portsmouth to see my mom and dad.

Bryan had finished his three-year commitment to pay back the scholarship money the army had given him to go through dental school. He was working as an associate for a dentist in Federal Way. His agreement wasn't paying him much, so he decided to take a risk and start his own practice.

David, age four, and Linda's mom and dad

Linda; Linda's mom; Linda's younger brother, Drew; and David, age four

David, age four, birthday

David, age five, cheering me on at a marathon, with David's godfather, Bob Williams, and his daughter Heidi

David, age four, enjoying ice cream with Granddad Joe (Linda's dad)

David with Mike and Kim Krattli

David, age five, building sandcastles on Daytona Beach with Granddad Joe and Grandma Hazel (Linda's parents)

David, age five, first boating trip on Ralph and Ian Stokes's boat

David, age five, with Bryan and Linda running in twelfth place at the 1982 Boston Marathon (time 2:48)

DAVID AGE SEVEN, STARTING PRIVATE PRACTICE, AND THE 1984 OLYMPIC TRIALS MARATHON

We borrowed money to buy our own two-thousand-square-foot condo office space at 18-percent interest in 1980 and built our own dental practice. For the first several years, we put any extra money we earned back into the practice and lived off my teaching salary.

We always prioritized and spent some money to travel back East to see my parents once or twice a year. Because Bryan was studying for his mastership in the Academy of General Dentistry (AGD), we traveled to other cities, like San Diego, Orlando, San Francisco, and New York, every summer for about a week to take courses or see the city. David always went with us.

In 1984, David was seven years old, and I took a year off from teaching high school chemistry to train for the 1984 Olympic Trials. This was the first women's

David, age six, taking the boat to the Statue of Liberty in New York

trials for the marathon in history, and I was one of five women who had a chance to qualify from Washington State. This was a huge goal for me.

David got to watch me train and try to qualify for the trials. The qualifying year was between May of 1983 and April of 1984, and the Olympic Trials was scheduled for May of 1984 in Olympia, Washington. We had a lot of interviews on TV and newspaper spots, so the pressure to qualify was intense. I would train, get injured, and train again too soon. Finally, in January of 1984, I took a rest.

QUALIFYING FOR THE OLYMPIC TRIALS MARATHON
I did end up qualifying for the Olympic Trials three months later in March by running the Emerald City Marathon in 2:50:59, just six weeks before the Olympic Trials. That year, David watched my struggle getting injured and getting back up, persevering in each race, and trying again.

David was at the finish line once again with Bryan to cheer me on. In May of 1984, at seven years old, David was in Olympia, Washington, watching the 297

David age 10

best women runners in the country run the Olympic trials. I finished that race in 2:47, which would have been in the top fifteen that summer at the LA Olympics if I had competed in that race. There were many TV shows and newspaper stories around the first women's marathon trials. David enjoyed the attention and was at the finish line of the trials to see history being made.

Chapter 2

DAVID'S FIRST SOLO FLIGHT

We tried to go east from Seattle to Portsmouth or Daytona Beach to visit my mom and dad at least once a year (they had a beach apartment in Daytona Beach). In 1984, when David was seven years old, I was training for the Olympic Trials and decided that I would send David out to my parents on his own—"unaccompanied," as the airlines called it. He would be flying United Airlines and would have to change planes in Chicago. We paid to have a flight attendant with him the whole trip and accompany him to the next flight in Chicago, which would land in Portsmouth, where Mom and Dad would pick David up. I was fine with this plan, and I explained to David what would happen during the two flights, Seattle to Chicago and Chicago to Portsmouth. David seemed fine to be flying on his own. I walked him onto the plane, and he got the "pilot wings" and all the special treatment. I thought I was fine until it was time for me to get off the plane.

Another mother was standing beside me, telling me about her experience when her son flew for the first time alone. She said, "He was fine until THEY FORGOT HIM." Of course, this shot me into a panic, and I cried the entire day until I heard from David and my parents nine hours later that David had arrived safely in Norfolk... David was fine—I was the one who was a wreck! Every night before bed, I would tell David, "I love you," to be sure—no matter what—he knew that I had a deep and unconditional love for him. There was nothing he could do to change that. Even if he behaved badly, I would say, "I may not like how you are acting, but I will ALWAYS LOVE YOU!" To this day, when David hangs up the phone or goes to leave, we still say "I love you" to each other. His heart is huge, and he has a sense for knowing how people feel that is very unique.

I have always told David I am VERY proud of him and that we were lucky enough to adopt him and have a choice to have him in our lives. I cannot imagine my life without our son. I often thank David's natural mother in my prayers for electing to have him and not have an abortion. My life and my husband's life are so much better because of her VERY unselfish decision. I have been driven to write David's story since he was very young for many reasons, but I wanted to wait until he was old enough to be OK with sharing his story. Many women cannot have children, and many women have them easily but choose to abort their baby. It is my hope that some women who might be driven to an abortion will by some miracle see "David's Story" and change their minds, thus enabling a couple or single parent to experience the blessings of "raising a child they did not make," like we did.

In 1985, David was in third grade, and he loved to perform. He had an amazing creative teacher named Mrs. Salisbury. That year he was in a performance called *Cinderfella*. He was a foot taller than all of his classmates, and watching the big boys dress up as Cinderella's stepsisters was a riot. David and two of the other tall boys were dressed up in fringe dresses and sang The Supremes song "Stop in the Name of Love."

David started to play soccer and basketball at age eight. We could tell by now that David would be very tall. He was so tall and lanky, sometimes he looked like he was running in slow motion. He wasn't initially very competitive, and during soccer drills, he would often run back to help the slow runners when they were running the field. David always loved others and tried to help them and continues to do so today. David's armspan was so wide even at eight years old that he was always put in the soccer goalie position. David begged me to let him play football, but because he was growing so fast, I was worried he would get hit in the knee cartilage and he would be damaged for life.

David, age eight, with first pair of skis

We knew David's natural mother was five feet, nine inches tall from the letter she gave us, but we did not know how tall his father was. David did play basketball at the YMCA almost year-round. In 1986, when David was nine years old, we bought a ski cabin at the top of chair seven on Crystal Mountain. We had started David in ski lessons at age eight and found he was a natural on the slopes and fearless.

David loved it when his great-uncle Eivind came to visit. Eivind and Great-Aunt Delores came to visit often. Eivind was my dad's "little" brother, who was six feet, three inches tall and was a three-star army general. They have two children, Jane and Chris, who are my cousins. We always had a taco-and-ice-cream-eating contest between David and Eivind when they came to town. They used a mixing bowl for the serving of ice cream.

As David got older, Bryan would take him out skiing on harder and harder runs. When he was eleven years old, we got him a yellow lab, who we appropriately

Uncle Eivind and David in a taco-and-ice-cream-eating contest

David picking out Niki

David, age fourteen, with Bryan and Linda at the top of Crystal Mountain

named Niki the Crystal Mountain Mogul Masher. Lois Deschner, another close friend who loves dogs, took David to dog training classes. I continued to train for marathons, and David went out on harder and harder ski runs with Bryan.

Soon David and Niki became inseparable. Niki loved the snow and would climb the mountain with me as I trained, only stopping if we saw a porcupine or other interesting wildlife. David was her alpha dog, though, and having Niki helped him by letting him be responsible for another being.

We rented two rooms of our cabin; one went to the ski team coach and his family, and the second to another family. The first room had triple bed bunks, and the second room had two double bed bunks. David and Bryan and I shared a third bedroom with a queen bed, and David slept on the floor in a sleeping bag. We had fifteen people living in the cabin, and often the whole ski team showed up to "hang out." Every Friday, right after school was out, our family drove up to the cabin full of skiers on the Crystal Mountain ski team.

Very soon, the ski coach put David on the team. Because of his size and weight, he was a natural for downhill racing, and the coach took him under his wing. We all crowded around the wood stove in the large rec room upstairs, with often twenty people or more at the large dining room table for meals. Watching my young son with his helmet on pointing straight down the ski slope so he could ski as fast as he could was, needless to say, VERY frightening for me—HIS MOM—but he loved the sport and did well.

Two of the skiers on this team actually made it to the Olympics. I was still competing in the marathon and 10k racing and had started to do Ironman training. The Ironman is a long-distance race starting with a 2.1-mile swim followed by a 112-mile bike ride, often in mountainous terrain, and finishing with a 26.2-mile run. We installed a treadmill in our cabin with a view of the mountain terrain, where I trained while David was at ski team practice and Bryan was out on the slopes.

When David, in seventh grade, I noticed he was having some trouble in math and reading and put him in Sylvan learning classes. I had taken a lot of courses in child development when I was getting my master in education, and I knew David was a little behind. I was also teaching and knew that kids who missed skills often had a hard time catching up later. David was very "street smart" and has a lot of emotional intelligence, but if he didn't get something right away, he became impatient. David can read how a person feels and is a great leader. I also know from research that often children who are growing rapidly, putting all their energy into growth, sometimes fall behind academically during these growth spurts. After a few months of concentrated learning, David accelerated to where he needed to be.

A NEW CHALLENGE FOR ME

I had also qualified to do the Ironman in Hawaii this year by winning my age group in a half-Ironman race. To train for the Hawaii Ironman race, I went up to Penticton, Canada, to do the Penticton Ironman in August 1987. David and Bryan came along and decided to do a rafting trip while I was racing. The race officials forgot to warn us that there were railroad tracks at the bottom of a steep hill ten miles into the race. I had taken aid at the rest stop at the top of the hill. When I saw the tracks, I braked with my left hand, which brakes the front wheel. I crashed, throwing myself off the bike. I broke three ribs, which cut me out of the Hawaii Ironman race, which was happening two months later, the following October, in 1987. Bryan realized how devastated I was, because this crash destroyed another goal I had worked for in athletics, which was to do the Ironman in Hawaii.

I was thirty-seven years old and had been teaching high school chemistry for eight years. David was ten years old. Bryan came home from work one day with another "life-changing" surprise for me. He handed me an application to dental school. I had been teaching honors chemistry at Auburn High School and had taken a course in computer simulation lab experiments through a summer program at NIH (National Institute of Health). I wanted to introduce computers into all the classrooms in Auburn High School but was getting pushback from the Computer Committee chair. Some said it might have been the cost, but I knew computers were the wave of the future, and I wanted to help my students. So I wrote a grant and went to the school board to ask for a $180,000 grant to accomplish this goal. I was also getting training on the Apple II computer and had been asked to go to Oregon to teach the Apple II course.

The computer chair was not happy that I had gone "above him" to get the job done, especially since I was a woman. Bryan had noticed my frustration of dealing with the school political system to make progress. So, given my athletic setback, Bryan thought this was great timing to get me to apply to dental school. David was ten.. Bryan had gone to the University of Washington Dental School admissions office and picked up an application. I was VERY surprised; I had given up the dream of going to dental school when we decided to raise David in 1977. I was thirty-seven years old. Did they even look at a person my age to admit into dental school? I went to the dental school to talk to Dean Omnell to see if they would even consider admitting someone who was ten to fifteen years older than the normal age to apply. He was very kind, and I found out that his wife, now an orthodontist, had also gone to dental school at a late age.

He encouraged me to apply and see what happened. Once again, Bryan's faith and love for me started us on a new and positive journey. I had graduated with a master of education and a zoology degree in 1973 with many, many credits. I had also taken college credits every year since to rise to a higher level on the teachers' pay scale. The dental application was due back East in three days. Never say anything is impossible—Bryan and I stayed up all night getting the materials together and found out we could put the application on a plane that would get it to the National Application Office back East overnight. You can apply to multiple dental schools, but because I was in Washington and I had a ten-year old son, I only applied to the University of Washington. We sent my application to the East Coast. It arrived on time. Then we waited.

About a month later, I received a call to have an interview at the University of Washington. I was VERY nervous and entered the room with a portfolio of job experiences and marathon and 10k races I had won. Another miracle of sorts happened when I discovered that my interviewer, Dr. Morton, was also training for some running races. We spent the next hour talking about training for running. The admissions office called about a month later to let me know I had been accepted into the University of Washington Dental School. Then I had to make a very tough decision.

My eleven-year-delayed dream of becoming a dentist was becoming a reality. This would be a major change to our life. I would be giving up a teaching job in honors chemistry, which I had worked toward for fourteen years, as well as my coaching. I would be entering into a very tough course of study and would have at least a sixty- to ninety-minute commute to the dental school each way if I lived at home, which was thirty-seven miles south of the dental school. David was ten and would be eleven when I started dental school. I talked to David about it, and he seemed excited. Bryan's mother had decided to retire, so she lived with us and helped David get to Scouts and sports activities. I could not have gone to dental school without her help. David loved her company and her grilled cheese sandwiches, and it gave her a chance to live with us and be with David. So we decided to "go for it."

DENTAL SCHOOL YEARS 1988–1992,
DAVID AGES ELEVEN TO FIFTEEN

As Ray Bradbury once said, "Sometimes you just have to jump off the cliff and build your wings on the way down." The work load was twelve- to sixteen-hour days, and I was often away at school from 6:00 a.m. until 10:00 p.m. David came with me to do lab work, often all weekend. He also spent a lot of time with Niki, our new puppy. We brought her home at ten weeks old, and she made short work of destroying the laundry room. It was David's responsibility to raise and train her.

David, Niki, Bryan, and I drove up to Crystal Mountain every weekend. The only way to get up to the cabin in the winter was by snowmobile or taking the chairlift. During the summer, there was a very narrow, winding road that an SUV could take up to the cabins. Niki would run under the chairlift while we took it up to the cabin. She was an amazing dog and would run up and down the mountain trail in the snow with me when David was training for the downhill racing. David and Niki were inseparable. Niki could retrieve a ball in a jungle and would not give up until she found the stick or ball you threw for her.

David was in Cub Scouts at age eight and Boy Scouts at age eleven. He loved to camp and earn badges. He continued to fly to Florida every summer to spend time with my mom and dad. Mom was the disciplinarian and Dad taught David how to check out girls on the beach and make jokes. It was these first experiences with flying, I believe, that got David interested in being a pilot. My dad was also a Coast Guard rescue pilot.

My first two years of dental school, no matter how busy I was, we would always go to the movies and Red Robin for dinner on Friday. David and I LOVE to go to the movies, and even today we go together to movies when we get a chance. David was very affectionate and always wanted to hold my hand. As he grew in height, this felt a little funny to me. At age thirteen, he was five-foot-eight, and I was five-foot-five.

Suddenly, what seemed like overnight, David decided he needed to be independent, and he became a teenager who did not want to be seen with his parents.

We would go to the mall to pick out clothes. He would go ahead of me to the stores, come back and let me know where his purchases were, and then I would go pay for them. The clothes I bought in June when he was thirteen years old and five-foot-eight were six inches too short in September of that year. David continued to grow off the charts. In his ninth grade year, when he was fourteen, he grew nine inches, from five-foot-eight to six-foot-five and wore sweats for the next couple of years.

My dental school schedule was tough. I would leave the house at 6:00 a.m.; drive the one- or two-hour (depending on traffic) commute from Federal Way to Seattle, where the dental school was; go to class all day; do lab work until 9:00 p.m.; and come home to see him in bed. During that growth spurt, I could actually see him getting longer each night. There were many days that I felt torn about being gone for so many hours a day, but David was getting a chance to know Bryan's mother, Laura, David's other grandma, well and they seemed to have fun together.

I could see David growing in his sleep my first year in dental school, and David also loved baseball

Linda and David age 15 at Linda's Dental School Graduation with Laura
(Bryan's Mom)

Gwen, Cousin Valerie, David and Linda

David #33 playoffs

David continued to play basketball, but I would not allow him to play football, even though the football coaches kept putting David on their teams. The coach would put him on the team, I would call the school and take him off the football team, and the coach would put him back on the football team again.

I graduated from dental school and joined our Federal Way dental practice in 1992, when David was fifteen and starting his sophomore year at Federal Way High School. He stopped skiing that same year, in tenth grade, because he was spending all his spare time playing basketball. The team practiced almost all year round. He played junior varsity as a sophomore and then varsity basketball as a junior and a senior. We spent much of our free time at either high school or Seattle Supersonics basketball games. Some of the best times we had were watching the NBA playoffs in Seattle or on TV. We spent several Mother's Day weekends watching Michael Jordon and Shaq in the NBA playoffs. David's Federal Way basketball team was ranked in the top three in the state.

David, age seventeen, bleached his hair

David's high school coach was Jerome Collins. As a sophomore, David was play-ing with several players on his team who ended up in the NBA after college. Because of the caliber of the players on the team, David did not get a lot of play-ing time as a sophomore. David was six-foot-eight and also had a great three-point shot. As captain of the team his senior year, he set a good example for other teammates who screwed up, and he often set them straight. There were times when David needed to be disciplined too. David was not really motivated to get good grades, so we decided to require him to get at least a 3.0 GPA to drive. He did come through with a 3.01 average.

Coach Collins, his basketball coach, was like a second father and held his players to a high standard. The team was always ranked in the top five in the state and almost won the state championships during David's sophomore year on the team. Bryan and I went to all the Sonics and high school basketball games and took David to practices at the PRO Club in Bellevue, where the Sonics team practiced.

David, age fifteen, running a "dog running race" with Niki

David also played and practiced with Michael Dickerson, who ended up playing pro basketball for several years. Because there were so many good players on David's team, his playing time was limited until he was a senior, but this experience was very valuable, and he still plays basketball with many of these classmates twenty-five years later.

Chapter 3

EAST COAST TOUR, 1993

During David's junior year in high school, we all went on an East Coast tour of New York, Pennsylvania, and Washington, DC, to go to plays and visit historical sites. His history teacher, Merlin Epp, and his wife, Jeanie, were another very positive influence in David's life, as were many of his teachers. Bryan and I took time out to be chaperones for the busload of juniors on the trip. We ate at Hard Rock Cafés and enjoyed great plays in all the major cities—a trip of a lifetime.

David, age seventeen, Varsity Basketball State Playoffs, center position, #33

TALL BOYS CUTTING TALL GRASS

When David was fifteen, he started his first creative business, "Tall Boys Cutting Tall Grass." He borrowed our Chevy truck and lawn mower and trimmer, traveled around to houses, and asked if they wanted their lawn mowed. David did very well that summer with his creative enterprise, along with two of his six-foot-six friends. They even had T-shirts. After that summer, David worked at a variety of jobs, including Sam's Club and Costco, stocking boxes and moving carts, and the Federal Way mall as a security officer. He even worked on the ramp for Alaska Airlines, loading bags. Because of his size and his smile and good-natured personality, he was very successful at getting work.

Throughout high school, David was popular, with a lot of girl friends and one steady girlfriend for several years. He always had a girlfriend and liked me to "bond" with them, meet them, and see if I liked them. I tried to be a good mom and "not give too much advice" unless asked, unless whatever I thought he was doing might be harmful to him or someone else.

David was a great son until he turned seventeen, and from seventeen to twenty-one, I used to tell him during this period that "I will always love you. I just cannot agree with your behavior right now." It seemed like there was some issue about every two weeks that we had to deal with—having parties when we were out of town without our permission and other things typical teenagers get into during this period we would just as soon forget… David never did anything really serious, like drugs or DUIs, just a few dumb things. Bryan and I were strict, and that seemed to pay off down the road. Sometimes kids just need to get "caught." He wasn't afraid of much, and I am not sure what he "got away with," but as a former high school teacher, I was very involved in being "nosy" about his friends and where he was. I often checked his room.

When he realized he wasn't going to play pro basketball, he seemed to lose interest and lose his way. Too many high school parents try to be their kids' "friends." Bryan and I were pretty strict and quick to discipline, even though David was almost a foot taller than Bryan. I was the "soft" parent, but when I got really angry. he knew what he had done was REALLY bad. Trying to be your child's friend

David's graduation, 1996, Federal Way High School

instead of their parent doesn't work when kids are in high school and junior high. I saw this firsthand when I was a high school teacher.

After high school, David attended junior college because he wanted to play basketball. He skipped classes at junior college and lied about it. The new basketball coach was mean and threw his players up against the wall as discipline. Most of the team quit. When David talks about this experience now, he says he felt lost and did not know what he wanted to do with his life. We took him aside and had a "tough love" discussion, saying, "We will fund your education to study anything you like—and go to any school you can get into—but you have to be committed." I always knew David was smart—he just wasn't driven until he found his true passion. His passion was flying, and his desire was to become a pilot like his Grandfather Johansen.

EMBRY-RIDDLE FLIGHT SCHOOL
David made his decision. Embry-Riddle in Daytona Beach, Florida, was his choice. This school has one of the best aviation programs in the country. We told David if he could get in, we would pay for his education and room and

board and he would not have any college loans. His education would be our gift to him.

He worked hard at getting recommendations and was admitted to Embry-Riddle in Florida. In 2000, I was VERY proud of him, and now the work began. He was twenty-three years old and seemed to be growing out of the "rough period" we experienced from seventeen to twenty-one years of age. We traveled to Florida and got him a small apartment, and we set up his kitchen with used furniture and dishes. For the next four years, he studied. He became serious about his passion and got his flying hours and his aviation degree.

We were so very proud of David as he went through graduation from Embry-Riddle and received his degree in aviation. My dad had passed away of brain cancer at age seventy-four, and we knew what a positive effect he'd had on David's decision to become a pilot. He would have been so proud, and I hope he is looking down on David today, watching him "soar."

David, age twenty-seven, graduating from Embry-Riddle Aeronautical University, 2004

The education at Embry-Riddle cost $250,000. In 2001, when the 9/11 tragedy hit the Twin Towers in New York, the aviation industry took a hit. We found out real fast that a career in aviation was not lucrative, and it took a long time to make any money.

DAVID'S FIRST FLIGHT JOBS, 2004

Spana flight was his first job as a pilot with an aviation degree. They paid him seventeen dollars an hour for flying as an instructor. The company only paid for the hours he actually logged in the air. When he was flying, he loved every minute. Some of the clients he served as a flight instructor to help them earn their private pilot or instrument rating licenses still stay in touch with him years later.

Next he progressed to a larger plane at Aero flight, a cargo company, and began accumulating his multi-engine hours. The next company was Airpac. This was also a cargo company. The planes were often old. On one trip, one of the wheels did not drop down when it was time to land. That was a huge scare and could have killed him, but he was able to control the landing.

He decided to move on to another company. Later that year, one of his friends died when his engine failed. Considering the risk young pilots take, the pay was minimal. Over the next few years, David received tremendous experience flying in mountainous terrain all over Alaska, Idaho, and Montana. He had to "boot off" the ice from his wings in cold weather. I asked him to give me a call or text me every few days so I could be sure he was OK.

Empire was David's next employer, which is a feeder company for FedEx and involved flying cargo in multi-engine planes over the mountains and into small Alaska and Montana cities. He was still flying solo as a single pilot. The pay was much better and he had good benefits, but considering his education cost us $250,000, it was frustrating that the companies did not pay more. Pilots say you are the best pilot you will ever be when you are flying as a single pilot and having to control the airplane without a lot of instruments. Having a job at Empire can also be rough because pilots are often away from home for several weeks at a time.

David, age twenty-six, after teaching a student to fly

As a mom, you hold your breath when your child is working in a job with tough weather and flying conditions that could kill him.

DAVID'S WIFE

For privacy reasons, David's wife has asked that I not put her name or his children's names in this book, so I will refer to her as David's wife, but it is not because I refused to call her by her first name like my dad did with Bryan. David met his future wife at a dinner with some of his friends in 2008. A week or so after this dinner, David called me and said he thought he had met "the one." I was thrilled!

A week or so after that, he called me again and said he wanted Bryan and I to meet her. There was one problem, though, he said. "She wants to live in California, and she doesn't want to have kids." I thought about it a minute—I knew David loved living in Washington, and he is our only child, so selfishly I wanted him close, and I knew he wanted to have his own children someday. He was terrific with kids. So I said to him, "Maybe you two need to have a conversation." They must have had the conversation, because they kept dating.

David, age twenty-seven, after aviation school, and David catching a 97-pound marlin on the Big Island

THE PROPOSAL, 2008

David was thirty-one at this time. We invited his girlfriend to my mom's condo in Daytona Beach to get to know her better. She was so smart and so decisive. His girlfriend was the fifth child out of six children in her family of four girls and two boys.

His girlfriend had lived in California, but when her father got ill with leukemia, she decided to come home and help care for him. She had lived with her older sister and her husband and their two children for a while and was great with kids. David asked her to marry him on that trip to Daytona, and I was so happy for him. He had waited a long time to find "the one," and you could tell they were very much in love. Because we only have one child, we told his girlfriend and David we would pay for the wedding and have a reception at our house a month later for all their friends. It was fun to work with her on the reception planning. She is very talented, decisive, and organized, and—best of all—you could tell they really loved each other. They got married on August 20, 2009, and decided to go to the Big Island of Hawaii and get married on the beach.

David's wife's dad's leukemia left him weak, and her parents could not travel, so we thought it would be better for just her and David to go to Hawaii on their own. The rest of the family met at our house, and the wedding was on a live video feed so we could see it in real time. David and his wife stayed in our condo on the Big Island for their honeymoon. We had a reception for all of their friends and our friends at our house in Federal Way in September 2009 with a Hawaiian theme.

My mom was eighty-three years old and made the trip out to Washington to be with us for the reception. We had over 125 people, put up a tent, and converted our yard and garage into a "Hawaiian Paradise." David's wife comes from a big family, and her mom and dad were at the reception, as well as many family and friends who had flown in from all over the country. We had a Hawaiian luau and over twenty hula dancers of all ages for entertainment.

Pictures from the Wedding

David and his new wife and hula dancers at Linda and Bryan's home, and
David and his new wife in Hawaii

Bryan, Linda, David, and Hazel (Linda's Mom and David's grandma

FIRST GRANDCHILD

David's wife was thirty-two and David was thirty-one when they got married. They decided it was best to try and get pregnant right away. She lost her first baby in the winter of 2010 to a miscarriage.

I remember the phone call from David like it was yesterday. My memories of my tubal pregnancies rushed back to me. That pit in my stomach and terrible feeling of loss hit me again. Although David's new wife did not have a tubal pregnancy, I knew how devastating the loss of a child can be. She seemed to recover quickly and got pregnant again right away. They decided not to find out whether the baby was a boy or a girl. She was due around the end of July or the beginning of August in 2011. In the middle of June, Bryan and I were at a dinner for the Washington State Dental Association in Seattle when we got the call that David and his wife had gone to the hospital, which was just a few blocks away from our meeting. We had just had dinner and gone to a movie with them the night before. Our grandchild wasn't due yet!

David's wife wanted us to wait a few days to come to the hospital. Our first grandchild was born seven weeks early, weighing about five pounds, on June 15, 2011. After two days, Bryan and I went to the hospital to see our new grandchild. I had a picture in my phone from the day we picked up David at three days old. I took a picture of our granddaughter, and you could hardly tell the difference between David's picture and hers.

I showed David the two pictures, and my big six-feet-seven-inches son started to cry. Growing up, David had my hair color and beautiful aqua eyes. Many people would say he looked like me with Bryan's big eyes, but they would always wonder where he got his height. I was five-foot-five, and Bryan was five-foot-ten—David was six-foot-eight with shoes on. I would laugh and tell people he got his height from all the pizza we ordered while I was in dental school. Then I would tell them David was adopted.

I was VERY proud of that and VERY proud of him. Now when his new daughter was three days old, David looked at her and it was like looking in a mirror. Her

3 day old picture was identical to David's picture when we picked him up from the hospital when he was 3 days old.

. . . She was in the ICU for a month as she developed, and David's wife made the thirty-minute trip to the hospital every day so their baby could have her breast milk and build up her immunity. The baby finally came home, and David's wife was exhausted. She was bearing most of the load, because David's job as a FedEx pilot kept him away from home for sometimes two weeks at a time. I tried to help her when I could get away from the dental office to give her a bit of a break, but the care was "all on her." It was a very stressful time, but our beautiful grandchild was thriving! Thanks to her amazing mom. Boy, was she thriving!

On her actual due date seven weeks later, she weighed nine pounds—every month she grew another size, and by the time she was two years old, she was in a size four. I continued to try to help as much as I could, but David's wife was exhausted most of the time. She had been working and going to school right after they were married. After she lost the first baby, they decided she should stay at home. Sadly, her dad passed away in October 2010, shortly before his great-grandchild was born. My dad had died of lung cancer that had metastasized to his brain in 1998 at the young age of seventy-four, so neither my dad nor David's wife's dad got to meet this first great-grandchild. David's wife was very close to her dad, so she had experienced a lot of losses in a short period of time.

She and David had rented a small apartment in Bellevue and were very happy. They were not sure whether or not they wanted to have another child, and I was trying to be a good mother-in-law and keep my mouth shut.

FIRST HOME AND NEW SURPRISE
They decided they wanted to own their own home and found a three-bedroom, one-and-one-half-bathroom rambler with a large fenced-in yard on a short sale. Short sales are where the home goes into foreclosure and you buy the home from the bank. They are tricky and don't often go through, but David and his wife were patient and closed the sale a few months later. We had them over for dinner in the spring of 2013. My granddaughter was two and a half and had a T-shirt on

Kona age 6- same age as 2nd granddaughter

that said, "I am going to be a BIG sister"… It took me a minute, but Bryan and I suddenly realized David's wife was pregnant again.

A few months before David's wife was due, we adopted a new golden retriever puppy named Kona. She was our fifth dog, with Niki, our yellow lab, being the first, and then four golden retrievers. We were so happy and really looking forward to our second grandchild.

SECOND GRANDCHILD

They decided not to find out whether they were having a boy or a girl and that they would be surprised again. I "held my breath" during the first trimester in hopes that all would go well. This pregnancy went much smoother, and our second grandchild was born on her due date.

David's Daughters   Grand kids 2021 Daytona Beach

My first granddaughter loved her little baby sister most of the time, but from my vantage point, it seemed she didn't quite know what to do with her until she got old enough to play with. David was thrilled and now had two beautiful daughters and a beautiful wife to spoil. David was still working for Empire Airline, the FedEx feeder. His wife stayed at home with the babies. David was still flying into Alaska and other mountainous terrain, which was difficult flying but great experience. David's wife was often "flying solo" as a mom, with a three-year-old and a new baby to care for. They did not live very far from us, so I was fortunate to be able to go see them when I could. I was still working full-time as a dentist. I was also an officer of the Academy of General Dentistry, which has forty thousand members, for eight years and served as president in 2014. I was flying close to 175,000 miles a year to meetings all over the country, as well as flying to Virginia every two weeks to help take care of my mom.

My grandchildren loved to have books read to them. David's wife always had many toys and books available for playtime and limited any TV or video viewing for several years. My oldest granddaughter loved Legos and had a talent for building some very complicated pieces, like a helicopter, at a young age. Both girls have tremendous ability to focus on what they are doing, and David and his wife have been terrific parents. They introduced both girls to swimming early, and my oldest grandchild was swimming like a fish without flotation devices by age three. They have been up to Crystal Mountain to ski, and David and his wife take the kids on all kinds of outings. We have been to Hawaii several times to stay in our condo on the Big Island. The girls love the beach and experiencing "Hawaiian food" at restaurants.

David and his wife and the girls have also traveled nonrevenue to Florida when space is available, because this is one of the benefits of David being a pilot. My mom left us her condo, which is right on Daytona Beach, when she passed away, and David has many wonderful memories, having spent many summers there with my parents, Joe and Hazel. Building sandcastles and swimming in the pool and the ocean were some of their favorite activities.

From 2012 through the fall of 2015, my mom, Hazel, was very ill. She lived in Virginia, which took me nine hours and two flights to get to. She had fallen in a doctor's office while waiting to be helped at the reception desk. Thank goodness the office was right next to the hospital, or the fall would have killed her. She cracked open her skull and had a brain bleed.

When I got the call, I contacted our caregiver in Portsmouth, Virginia, and got on a red-eye flight to Virginia that night. Mom was in the ICU for a month. I was with her most of the time, and my brothers Bruce and Drew and Bruce's wife, Pat, also came to Virginia.

CARING FOR MOM

We took shifts in the ICU. It was amazing to me that at times there was only a receptionist in the ICU. Mom was having trouble breathing, and I pointed it out to the nurse. I sat with her that day and felt there was probably something wrong. I asked the nurse to contact the pulmonary doctor, and instead they brought in a machine for her to blow into. This was having no positive effect. Finally I insisted that I see the doctor and told them I was a dentist and I knew there was something wrong. Twenty minutes later, a pulmonary doctor came in—he looked at her and rolled her into surgery. Her lungs were filling with water and she could hardly breathe. It was then that I realized how important it is to have an advocate for your loved one in the ICU.

Having said this, in general the nurses were terrific, and they had to do everything for her. Staying in a bed leaves a person very weak, and Mom was sent to rehabilitation for six weeks to get strong enough to walk again. She was eighty-six years old. Just a few years before that, Mom had flown out to see us, and now she needed assisted living care. I was working in my dental practice full-time, president of the Academy of General Dentistry, and flying back East from Seattle to Portsmouth, Virginia, to care for Mom every two weeks with the help of my brother Drew, who would drive down from Pennsylvania to help out. Bruce and Pat, Bruce's wife, also flew from Omaha, Nebraska, to help. Drew and I would alternate going out to see Mom in Virginia and be with her. Her house was about a mile from the assisted living facility she was living in, and we had also hired a wonderful caregiver, Connie, to be our "boots on the ground" when we were not able to be with Mom.

Assisted living facilities promise you that your loved one will be checked on by an attendant every two hours—even at night. We found out, however, that this was not the case when Mom fell one night going to the bathroom and could not get up. She was too far from the cords they have you pull on the walls to get help. The rug was an industrial grade, and Mom struggled for over four hours trying to get up, which caused severe rug rash that landed her in the hospital with severe skin adhesion and infections.

Needless to say, I was very discouraged. I canceled my patients and flew out to Virginia to check on her. David had called me on the cell phone when I got there to see how I was doing. David seemed to always know when I needed some encouragement. I started crying over the phone from the constant worry and stress created by my mom's hospitalization and all my other responsibilities.

David decided to fly across the country from Washington State to Virginia, and the next day, he showed up at Mom's front door—unexpected, and what a surprise it was! I was so happy to see him and knew his wife had encouraged him to come out and support me for a few days, even though it meant she would have to take care of the grandkids on her own. He had taken a "nonrev" flight out to Washington, DC; rented a car; and driven four hours to Portsmouth. This is just the kind of person David is. When you need help or emotional support, he is there, no matter what the obstacles are. I cannot express how much this meant to me. During this stressful time of caregiving for my mom, David did this a lot. The nice thing about Empire was that even though David was gone a lot, when he was home he had a lot of time off.

A NEW CHALLENGE APPLYING TO WORK AS A COMMERCIAL AIRLINE PASSENGER PILOT

In early 2015, David and his wife decided they were tired of David's cargo-flying schedule, because he was often gone for over two weeks at a time. He decided to apply with the airlines to fly passengers in 737 planes throughout the United States. This was a tough decision, because Empire had been good to them and the competition to get hired was fierce. He had an interview that he thought had gone well in early 2015. He was thirty-eight years old and had a lot of flying hours. They call you into the interview in groups, and only a few people get hired. He did not make it that winter, and applicants are encouraged to wait a year to apply again, but he decided to get some "interview coaching" and try again in a few months. David's wife was VERY supportive of David's dream too.

He was granted another interview in another group a few months later. By then I was past president of the Academy of General Dentistry, and Bryan and I were in Chicago waiting to fly back to Washington State from a meeting. We were sitting in an airport restaurant and received the call from David.

"I got the job!" he exclaimed. Bryan and I were beaming! We were so proud of his persistence! David had to wait several more months before he actually started, and Empire was excited for this new opportunity for him. They allowed him to continue to fly for them until he actually started with the commercial airlines… We were all ecstatic! David would go through extensive training and testing with the FAA in flight simulators before he did any actual flights.

There were many computerized tests and frequent simulation tests. David came down to our house to study for days so he could have concentrated quiet time. I have never seen him work so hard and want something so bad. A job as a commercial airline pilot was, as he described it, "living his dream," and he looked so very handsome in his uniform too! I would quiz him using cards with terms and flight situations I did not understand. But the answers were on the backs of the cards, and David responded with all the answers perfectly. I remember David calling us after one stressful test. He had taken his test, and the instructor called him up to the front of the room, as David described, with a stern look—then smiled and told him he had received 100 percent.

You had come a long way, DAVID! Here you were, a first officer working for a great airline! On top of that, Bryan and I now get flight privileges.

Your dad and I cannot describe in words how very proud we were to watch you as you have grown into an amazing man, husband, and father. This is part of the reason I wanted to write this story. If by some miracle David's biological mother sees this book and reads it, she will know this is her son and she made the right choice entrusting Bryan and me to raise him.

The following months were exciting for David and the family. The first year, you are on probation, making 40 percent of your pay, so their budget was very tight. I helped out whenever I could by buying the kids clothes and other things they needed. My oldest grandchild was four and continuing to grow very fast. She was in a size eight by now, and her sister was one and had blonde hair and blue eyes. She looked just like David's baby pictures.

CARING FOR MOM IN 2015

I was continuing to work as a full-time dentist, was past president of the Academy of General Dentistry, and continued to fly back to Virginia to help care for my mom. We had decided to move Mom back to her home in Portsmouth, Virginia, and hire round-the-clock full-time caregivers, with shifts of eight hours each. The assisted living care was costing us $5,500 dollars a month, and we were not happy with the care she had received there. Mom could walk with the aid of a walker but could not get out of her chair without help. Drew, my younger brother, and I would alternate caring for her every two weeks, and my brother Bruce and his wonderful wife, Pat, also came out a few times to help when he could get away from his teaching responsibilities at the University of Nebraska in Omaha.

I was still traveling a lot to dental meetings around the country because of my national position with the Academy of General Dentistry. In the summer of 2015, Mom had taken a turn for the worst. Mentally, she was as sharp as ever, but her heart rate would often slow to a dangerously low level. She would get very weak, and we had to visit the emergency room several times during my visits. Connie was still our "boots on the ground" and would call me if she felt I needed to come out sooner than was scheduled. In October 2015, on one of my visits, I had rushed Mom to the hospital in an ambulance again because her heart rate and blood pressure had suddenly plummeted. When the doctor came in to give her the test results, she sat up in bed and said, "I am tired of playing this game." We had already had the difficult talk about dying, which was very, very hard for me.

Bruce and Pat had also talked to Mom about dying during their last visit a few weeks before. Mom was one of the most kind and caring people I knew. I would not have accomplished all I had in my life without our weekly calls and her encouragement. When I lost the babies in 1976, she was there for me. When we were given the gift of adopting David, she took him in as her own and often "straightened him out" on his long summer visits to Florida with Mom and Dad at their condo. I could not imagine life without her. The hospice nurse came in to explain how the medications worked, and we all agreed this was the best thing to do for Mom's sake. Mom was still very sharp mentally and seemed to know what was happening. We were staying in her home, and the next two weeks were heart-wrenching for all of us as she continued to decline. I was awake most of the time.

I wanted to be with her at the end and could not remember when I had last had much sleep. I had held the medical power of attorney for my best friend, who died at age fifty-four of breast cancer, and had gone through the stages of dying with my dad's brain cancer, so I knew the signs. My brother Drew came down to Portsmouth with his family. David called again when we made the decision to start hospice care. As always, he was my rock. I knew it would be tough for David to get away, since he was new at his job flying for the airlines. Bryan, my husband, was handling his patient load as well as mine at our dental practice. I was in Mom's house, caring for her with the nurse. I knew she did not have much time left because she was sleeping a lot and not eating, and her skin and nails were beginning to look gray. Mom would smile, hug me, and tell me she loved me. My breath would get stuck in my throat as I maneuvered through those last few weeks, still not able to fathom what life would be like without her.

She was always there, and I was so thankful I had made the effort to be with her so much those last few years. You never know how much time you have left with someone you love. We need to cherish each day! When I am having a tough day, I still find myself wishing I could pick up the phone and get her counsel. That after-noon, there was a knock on Mom's door. I had not been expecting anyone, but when I opened the door, there was my son, David, and my four-year-old granddaughter. Once again, as a surprise, David had flown six hours to Washington, DC; rented a car; and driven for four hours to see me, knowing I needed the support at this very tough time. He gave me a big hug and said, "How are you doing, Mom?" I started to cry, and he took me into his big bear arms, just knowing how tough things had been.

Mom woke up and recognized David, and she recognized her great-granddaughter.

She was able to see her great-granddaughter for the first time. I did not think she had much time left and was so happy David had come out at this crucial time for me. His wife gave up a lot to have him come out and leave her home with the baby, so I was very thankful. That is the kind of person David is—every phone call ends with "I love you, Mom," and he thanks Bryan and me all the time for helping him reach his dream job of flying on a major airline. I am so glad he has had the joy of a family of his own and is close enough for us to see each other. David is a great husband and father and a very, very special son. That night I stayed up with Mom and the caregiver who had come for the night shift. My brother's whole extended family had come over to see Mom, my granddaughter, and David.

We had given Mom a sleep aid to help her sleep. We had not used any of the morphine supplied by hospice yet, although the nurse had said it was OK. I had been up for two days, so I decided to get a few hours of sleep. David and my granddaughter had gone to bed. They were exhausted from the trip. The caregiver woke me up a few hours later and told me Mom did not seem to be breathing. I checked her and realized she was gone. We had said our "goodbyes," but it was still so very hard to believe Mom had passed away.

Mom used to say, "I want to have lived so that when I am gone, people will think well of me." David spent a lot of time with Mom on his visits to Daytona and Portsmouth every year. She always modeled kindness and caring and was a rock for all of us as we were growing up. She will always be in our hearts. I miss her every day.

Wow—there is no describing the feeling of losing your mom. I wish I had been there holding her hand when she passed, but I was glad it was in her sleep and I was so, *so* glad David had made it in time to see her… one last time. It was 4:00 a.m., and I woke David up. I needed him—he sat there with me and gave me a big hug. David was very close to Mom too. He had spent many summers with Mom and Dad growing up, in Virginia with Buffy, their dog, and driving to Daytona Beach to the condo. We sat there for a while and finally called my brother Drew, who came right over. We called the hospice nurse and the funeral home and were able to make plans to bury Mom at Arlington National Cemetery. My uncle General Eivind Johansen had been able to get burial plots next to my dad so that

Mom would be buried with Dad and Delores, Eivind's wife, would be buried with him. Their plots are very close to where President Kennedy is buried.

MORE TOUGH NEWS IN 2015

David and my granddaughter got in the rental car and headed back to DC and the long plane ride home to Seattle. After Mom's funeral and service at the Methodist Church in Portsmouth, Virginia, I headed home to Washington to get back to my dental practice. While caring for Mom, I realized I had been very stressed and sleep-deprived. In October of 2015, during those last weeks of caring for my mom, what looked like a canker sore had appeared on my lower lip. The canker sore would not heal. It would scab over and then come back. As a dentist, I knew it was unusual for a canker sore not to heal and continue to come back right away. I also had never had canker sores before. I went to my dermatologist, and she gave me some lip medication but did not recommend a biopsy.

One month later, in November 2015, there was no improvement, so I had an oral surgeon who was a friend do the biopsy. She rushed the results and called me within a few days. The biopsy results showed squamous cell carcinoma on my lower lip. It had been quite a year with all that happened with my mom, and now this. I could not go back to the practice after I heard the news. I was shaking… I called Dr. Truelove at the University of Washington to ask him to recommend a surgeon for me. I went to a specialist for head and neck surgery at the University of Washington. The specialist said we would have to have the cancer removed. My mom's funeral at Arlington National Cemetery was in February 2016, and I would not be able to fly after the surgery, so I had to wait until early March to see how much of my face would be removed. I knew survivors who had lost half their jaw from squamous cell carcinoma… but I thought I had caught it early.

He did not know if my whole lower lip would be removed until we did the procedure. The procedure takes two days. A Mohs surgeon, who is a specialist in skin cancers and surgery, removes the cancer and tests the area to see if all the cancer cells were removed. In my case, they had to go in twice and ended up having to remove almost the whole lower lip. This part was done with me awake, with a local anesthetic in the lip. They were able to save the lip's border, which made it easier to reconstruct. The next day I was put to sleep, and a head and neck surgeon took tissue from inside my mouth and reconstructed the lip. I had forty-two stiches and was bandaged, so I did not know what I would look like. I did not want anyone to see me, especially the grandkids, and I had told David and his wife about the procedure, but I did not want them to see me either.

Even though I was bandaged, I did not want to scare my grandchildren or have them see me look so ugly. I had no idea what part of my face would be removed. I only missed a few days of doing dentistry at the office, because I was able to wear a mask. The day I got home from the reconstruction, David and his wife called, and David showed up at my door with a Frosty, which is a thick, soft ice cream from Wendy's. I am so glad he came, even though I had told him not to come. I really needed the emotional support! I often think, "What would my life be like if David's mom had aborted him and he wasn't in my life?"... Bryan had been with me for the two days during the surgery. Once again I got a big hug from my son, who has always been there for me during the toughest times, and this *definitely* was one of them!

First losing my mom in October, and now lip cancer a few months later... Wow, 2015 was another one of those years I could easily forget. Life has a habit of lifting us back up after we get slammed into the ground. I have lived long enough to realize that after every tragedy there is often a triumph!

We had also been approached by a dentist who wanted to buy our practice in December of 2015. With my getting cancer and Bryan becoming the president of the Washington State Dental Association, our friend's timing could not have been better, even though we had not been looking to sell.

David and Bryan and I traveled to the East Coast in February of 2016 to bury my mom at Arlington National Cemetery with my dad and next to my uncle, General Eivind Johansen. Bruce and Pat and Drew and Gwen and their family were also there.

By now, David had finished his year of probation at the airlines and had a bigger paycheck every month. His wife had decided to homeschool the girls, and they were still living about forty-five minutes from our home. The flight schedule was much better, with the longest trips taking him away for at most four to five days. I spent time at least once a week going up to see his wife and the grandkids, and David when he was home. The scars from my cancer surgery had healed, although my lower lip remained numb and the lip was very thin. I was fortunate we found the cancer before it spread. The summer of 2016 was right around the corner, along 'with the hope for a better year and a less trauma-filled life.

David loves the 4th of July, and since our house was on the water, we had a mixture of David's friends and our friends over every year. David bought all the food, grilled hotdogs and hamburgers, and supplied the fireworks that they lit off on the beach just below our house.

I was enjoying working part-time at the dental office and having more time to see the grandkids and finally getting to some house projects that had been put off for ten years. Bryan was getting more involved in investing and had been elected to the National Academy of General Dentistry as speaker of the House. Our second granddaughter was two and getting a spunky personality of her own. She was not going to let her older sister take her toys or get all the attention. Our second granddaughter looked exactly like David's pictures from when he was that age—blonde hair and big blue eyes. Our oldest granddaughter was still growing fast and was wearing a size ten at age five. She is very meticulous and loves to work on the computer and build things. Her hair was becoming a dark brown like David's wife's, and she also had big blue eyes like both of her parents. Our oldest granddaughter loved swimming more than anything else and would swim for hours in the pool in Hawaii and at Daytona Beach.

Our second granddaughter was also loving the pool and copying her sister. She loved to jump off things and do somersaults all over the house. She started in a new sport called jiujitsu, a Japanese system of unarmed combat and physical training. She was so cute in her little black *gi*, which is the "uniform" they were required to wear: a cotton top and pants and her white belt, which communicated her rank with stripes. Our second granddaughter was also getting tall for her age and at age three years old was starting to wear a size five. Our first granddaughter's personality was a little more careful; she loved to read and do puzzles on her iPad. Our second granddaughter was all about running and running some more. And drawing—she loved to draw a picture and wrap it up with a bunch of Scotch tape to present us with a present from her. Bryan and I spent a day putting together a giant dollhouse for the girls.

We had an addition put above our garage with a large bedroom and a bathroom with a Jacuzzi bathtub for the girls and our guests to stay in if they spent the night. They loved that bathtub and stayed in it for hours. Both girls are very affectionate and gave hugs and kisses before bed and when they would leave. By then, our dog Kona was also three years old, the same age as our second granddaughter, who was showing an interest in her. Our first granddaughter had developed some allergies to nuts and dog hair and saliva and so could not pet the dog, but she used to put gloves and a jacket with a hood and long pants on just so she could go downstairs with Kona. Since that time, her allergies have gotten better, and my grandkids and I love to go downstairs to watch a kids' movie with popcorn and cuddle with Kona. When David was home from flying, he would give his wife a break and take us all to Denny's—one of our favorite places for breakfast. It is amazing the amount of food growing girls can eat! David's wife started them early on organic foods, and they eat all their vegetables and have learned to bake with healthy ingredients.

In 2018, at age seven, our oldest granddaughter began to show a real interest in horses and was taking lessons every week on a big ranch on Mercer Island. She also loved to help gather the chicken eggs and decided when she "grew up," she wanted to own her own farm. She was still swimming regularly. David's wife continued to homeschool the girls, and it was fun to watch them create and act out stories together. Both girls are very affectionate and love to climb into Mom's or Dad's or my lap to have stories read or just to cuddle.

In 2017, Bryan was going to run in an election for the American Dental Association (ADA) Board of Trustees. This is a group of about twenty-two dentists who help make policy for all of dentistry in the United States and the world. The trustee term was four years and would start in 2018. We were on our third year of working part-time in the dental practice we had sold in 2016.

Bryan and I had taken several courses with David's wife on flipping homes to resell, and I was in Hawaii for a week working on a home we were rehabbing to flip. Bryan was home in Washington attending some dental meetings. He called me in Hawaii and said, "Remember how I was going to run for ADA Trustee this year (2017)?"

"Yes," I said.

Bryan paused and then said, "Well, I think you should run. You would have a better chance to win. I called a few friends who were delegates who would be voting in the trustee election, and they all said to go for it."

David, his wife, and the kids living with Bryan and Linda, 2018–August 2020

It was May 2017, and the election was in September of that year. I ended up winning the election, and the trustee job started in October of 2018. I told David and his wife this position of trustee would require a lot of travel all over the US, to Chicago and my five states (Oregon, Washington, Idaho, Montana, and Alaska), and Bryan and I would be gone a lot.

The real estate market was doing very well in Washington State and across the country. David and his wife had done a lot of work to upgrade the home they had lived in and decided to sell it. They asked Bryan and I if they could move into our house and live with us for a while—maybe a year—so they could clear their house out while they were trying to sell it and not be pressured to buy another home in an inflated real estate market. I was thrilled. My job as trustee would have me gone from home about half the days during the next four years, and I would see a lot more of my grandkids if they lived with us. Ages five and eight were the perfect time to have the kids around. David and his wife and my two grandchildren moved all their things into our garage and other rooms.

This arrangement, with no mortgage owed on a home, would allow them to save money to put down on their next home and maybe do some things they could not otherwise afford, with free travel through David's job. David's wife and the girls went to the Dr. Seuss exhibit near Detroit, and their whole family went on a cruise in the Caribbean. They also came out to Hawaii with us. In the spring of 2020, after living about a year with us, they started to look for a home with a water view to buy. In March 2019, Bryan and I had flown out to Hawaii to get our condo ready for some renters to come on March 15. The COVID-19 virus had just hit Washington State, and we ended up getting "stuck" on the Big Island until the end of May.

David and his wife found a home with a beautiful view, an acre of woods, a lot of privacy, and plenty of room for the children to play and plant a vegetable garden and fruit trees. The house had windows surrounding it on all sides and had been upgraded with some nice finishes. There was some work to do on the roof and deck, and they negotiated a good price on the sale. They are about forty-five minutes to an hour from us with good traffic. David would have a longer commute to

Grandkids on Daytona Beach

Grandkids in front of Bryan and Linda's house

work at Sea-Tac airport, but they felt it was worth it. The girls could safely go bike riding or play safely in the yard. They each have their own bathroom and private space. After sharing a room with their parents for a year and a half in our house, this was VERY exciting for both of them.

THE FUTURE

This is where I will end my story about my son, David, and the miracle that happened to bring him into our family. When you reach almost the seventh decade of life, you realize life is full of triumphs and tragedies, but the future is always bright if you make the most of what you have. When "stuff happens," you pick yourself up and go on, because there is often a rainbow after the storm. I was driven to write this story to share with others how wonderful it can be to adopt a child and "raise a child you did not make" and help to "heal a heart you did not break." I am

"Linda and Bryan at ADA Trustee Dinner 2019

88

hoping that David's natural mother will find it and know David is having quite a life and that he will have many more years of wonderful experiences.

I wanted to wait until David was old enough to want his story told. He did not want to try to find his biological mom or two older brothers, because he did not want anyone to get hurt. Sometimes that journey does not end well. At forty-four years old, however, he wanted this story told in case another "miracle" happens and his mother or two older brothers see or hear of the book. Perhaps they may want to seek him out. He would be excited to finally meet his biological mom and two older brothers, but only if they felt comfortable meeting him.

David's birthdate and the location of the birth hospital are on the cover. If you find yourself reading this story and want to help David's natural mother find him, please take a picture of the cover and put it on social media to help.

To David's natural mother:

"Thank you for giving me David." I hope someday you will know what a difference you made in our lives.

Thank you to my brother Bruce Johansen, who helped me with the book and has written and published over forty-five books himself. Thanks to Bob and Linda Williams, who also helped me with the book's history. They have been David's godparents for over forty years.

CPSIA information can be obtained
at www.ICGtesting.com
Printed in the USA
BVHW050626220721
612426BV00019B/893